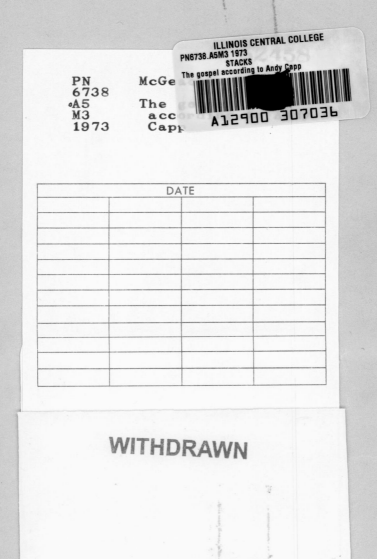

DATE		

the GOSPEL ACCORDING TO ANDY CAPP

D. P. McGeachy, III
FOREWORD BY ROBERT L. SHORT

JOHN KNOX PRESS
Richmond, Virginia

Scripture quotations from the *Revised Standard Version of the Bible* are copyrighted 1946 and 1952; from *The New Testament in Modern English*, © J. B. Phillips 1958.

The excerpt beginning on page 20 is reprinted with permission of Macmillan Publishing Co., Inc., from *The Last Battle* by C. S. Lewis. © C. S. Lewis 1956.

Cartoons are used by arrangement with Publishers-Hall Syndicate, New York, and are copyrighted, © Daily Mirror Newspapers Ltd., London.

Library of Congress Cataloging in Publication Data

McGeachy, D   P
    The gospel according to Andy Capp.

    "Scripture quotations from the Revised standard version."
    Includes bibliographical references.
    1. Smythe, Reginald. Andy Capp. 2. Comic books, strips, etc.—Moral and religious aspects.
I. Title. II. Title: Andy Capp.
PN6738.A5M3 1973   741.5'942   73-5347
ISBN 0-8042-1955-9

© John Knox Press 1973
Printed in the United States of America

To
ALICE
for putting up with 'er own 'andicap

FOREWORD

One of my favorite *Andy Capp* cartoons goes like this:

FLO   (*on her way out of the house*): I'm off t' the Institute, Pet—There's a lecture on social relations.

ANDY   (*in front of the telly with a "pint"*): Yer wastin' yer time, Kid—People are 'opeless.

FLO   (*shouting*): What yer talkin' about—YOU'RE people!

ANDY: Well—?

FLO   (*Stops and considers. Then returns, removing her coat*): Anythin' decent on telly?

Indeed, Andy Capp *is people.* This is not only why Andy is so disturbingly easy for all of us people types to identify with, but it is also why he is so theologically significant. For Andy *is* people not as we would like ourselves to be, but he is people just as we really are. Martin Luther once remarked that Original Sin is like a wound from which men never fully recover. Or, as any bloke from the English Midlands might put it, "Original Sin is like 'aving a permanent 'andicap." And therein lies the pun that tells us who *we* or *Andy Capp* or *people* really and truly are: we are all people who come *originally* into life without faith in God, not only a handicap extremely difficult to overcome but also a deficiency that causes all sorts of tragicomic behavior in the meantime.

But among all us people, it is especially the *churches* who, for two closely related reasons, should be especially grateful to

Reginald Smythe for creating Andy Capp. First, for almost two decades now, the churches and their theologians have gone to unbelievable lengths in trying to track down "Modern Man," "Secular Man," "Man Come of Age"—that is, today's man self-confidently sure of himself and therefore with no need of a "heavenly Father." They want to learn as much as they can about this typical "outsider" in order to better "communicate" with him. But if the theologians had only "unstuffed" themselves long enough to read the comics occasionally, they might have saved themselves a lot of trouble. For Modern Man is alive and well in Andy Capp if nowhere else. Just ask yourself—who better than Andy Capp fits the great Karl Barth's description of "Modern Man" as a man who *thinks* he's come of age but "proves daily" that he hasn't?

The second reason is like unto the first, for Andy himself is constantly doing his part to puncture and unstuff the pomposities and self-righteous presumptions of the churches. "Ah, Mister Capp! Just the lad I want t' see!" says the "vicar," looking down his nose at Andy. (In *Andy Capp,* always read "church" for "vicar.") "We 'aven't seen much of you at church lately," he pontificates, careful to use the pontifical "we." Replies Andy: "If it comes t' that, we 'aven't seen much of you in the snooker room either." "I'll 'ave t' pull me socks up!" mumbles the vicar, sheepishly slinking away and looking a bit more human.

Why is *Andy Capp* so popular at just this time? It is tremendously funny, of course. But again it is probably the *honesty* of the strip that gives its humor not only its broad universality but also the strong appeal of depth. It appeals to both the "inner man and the outer woman," as Andy would say. Garry Trudeau, the young creator of the very fresh and popular *Doonesbury* comic strip, has recently said in an article on the comics: "The fact of the matter is that a world-weary public is now amused only by representations of despair more agonizing than its own."* Or, as Flo cheerfully remarks, after anxiously waiting up for Andy only to overhear the sobs of the woman next door, "There's nothin' so consolin' as findin' that your neighbour's troubles are at least as big as your own!"

In *The Gospel According to Peanuts* we learned, to quote Linus, that "the theological implications alone are staggering." This time around it may be Andy himself who is doing the staggering; but that there are still theological implications aplenty, this charming little book clearly shows.

Robert Short
Author of *The Gospel According to Peanuts*

---

* "Maggie & Jiggs & Blondie & Dagwood & Lucy & Charlie," *Couples* (New York: The New York Magazine Press, 1973), p. 33.

CONTENTS

1.
Unlikely Beginnings

The gospel has a way of arriving in the hands of surprising messengers. It is delivered by tax collectors and fishermen, and even by precocious children and a talking beagle. But there is no more astonishing evangel than Andy Capp. He is the unlikely hero of a comic strip that began a decade ago in the London *Daily Mirror* and rapidly spread throughout the world. Apparently readers identify with him. Istanbul's *Hareket Gazetesi* editorialized:

> Andy is as much Turkish as he is English, and he is probably Greek, Italian and Polish too. Our readers got addicted to him in a week. As one of them put it, he is what every man wants to be in his spare time.[1]

But why would anyone want to identify with Andy Capp?

> He is a 5-ft. 4-in., 46-year-old, potbellied, wife-beating little lay-about. His floppy cap not only hides his eyes but never comes off—either in bed or on his rare visits to the tub. A cigarette is permanently glued to his lip. His bulbous nose glows whenever he has a snootful, which is nearly every night. He has no discernible trade and lives on the dole as if he had earned it. He is selfish, improvident, coarse, arrogant and bullying.[2]

That being the case, what's so funny? Why do *I* identify with him? What is there about him that causes another Capp to call Reginald Smythe, his creator, "the most popular English humorist with Americans since Charles Dickens"?[3] He goes on to say:

> In one major respect, Smythe differs from Dickens, and from most of the popular humorists who have preceded him. In the

world of Dickens, and of most humorists, there is nobility and sentiment amid the laughter. If there is none but ludicrous sentiment or hypocritical nobility in his comic characters, Dickens and our Twain and Spain's Cervantes comfort us with other characters, or other aspects of the same characters, possessing noble sentiments. There isn't a shred of nobility in Smythe's characters, or of sentiment.[4]

If he is indeed so devoid of that which is admirable, why do I not gnash my teeth when I read him, or at best turn away in disgust? Why, in heaven's name, do I laugh with delight? And above all, what makes me like Andy Capp?

I like him not because he is the ideal that I want to be, but because (*horribile dictu!*) he is what I am. And it comforts the sinner in me to know I'm not alone.

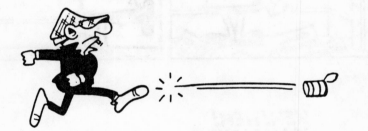

Smythe has captured more than the character of the industrial neighborhood in northern England where he grew up; he has got hold of the authentic human predicament. No wonder that we laugh; we have to!

Laughter is the chaser that lets life's bitter drink go down a little easier. It is a weapon against despair. When we can laugh at ourselves, or even a literary projection of ourselves, like Andy, then we are on the verge of discovering the humility that can save. This is part of what Jesus meant when he said, "How happy are the humble-minded, for the kingdom of Heaven is theirs!" (Matthew 5:3, Phillips).

There are two ways of looking at humanity, both of which have biblical support yet seem to stand in opposition to each other. One is the optimistic view that man is "in the image of God" (Genesis 1:27). He is thus only a "little less than God" (Psalm 8:5). Building on this base, without the corrective of the other, many humanitarian dreams have been constructed, some of them naive and most of them doomed to disappointment.

In this view, man, along with the rest of creation, is basically good (Genesis 1:31), and it provides the foundation for authentic humanism. Those who hold to it exclusively criticize all the prophets of doom, from clergymen to psychiatrists, for loading us with guilt feelings and stifling the "free expression of selfhood." They would say: "The first assertion to make about man is that he is good. Sin is merely a flaw in what is basically sound and right."

The other viewpoint sees goodness as the unusual miracle and sin as the natural state of things. Ever since man first tried to "be like god" (Genesis 3:5), the most fundamental thing you can say about him is that he is sinful:

> All have sinned and fall short of the glory of God. . . . None is righteous, no, not one. [Romans 3:23, 10]

On this base can be built a monumental pessimism, from Ecclesiastes through Omar to Sartre. Here we are, caught in this endless round and round, with no exit. When carried to its ultimate extreme, this view of man is called the Doctrine of Total Depravity. That does not mean (I am told) that everything and everybody is totally and completely depraved in every part, but that sin permeates all of our lives, and that no part of us is completely free from evil.*

----

* Except, of course, for writers and other completely objective authorities.

Andy Capp is authentic man. There is both good and bad in him, as there is in each of us. He has strengths that remind us that he is created in the image of God, and he has faults that shout of his human predicament as fallen man. He contains both grandeur and misery.

Granted, sometimes the grandeur is a little hard to see in Andy Capp. But so is it in the rest of us. The sins of the world shriek out; virtues need advertising. You only need to ask yourself what will get on the front page of a newspaper to remember that our sins overwhelm us. This is so not only because it is sin that gets the attention, but because, for the time being at least, it seems to have the upper hand. The Dark Powers are still on the offensive. In military terms, the moral struggle is about at Dunkirk, and the little beachhead that the forces of Love have made has not yet attracted much attention.

Since the wicked side of Andy is the most obvious (and maybe the most interesting), we will start with that. For that matter, I think Andy would approve of our beginning with his vices. While his life is not totally devoid of virtuous acts, it would not be an overstatement to say that his heart is not in them.

2.
Andy the Sinner

George Bernard Shaw, in *Don Juan in Hell,* describes the afterworld as containing a free passageway between heaven and hell. Don Juan, after looking the Devil's domain over for a while, decides he simply doesn't like it there and transfers to the other side of the gulf. This is not bad theology. It may be presumptuous to design the geography of eternity, but it is certainly true that the ultimate judgment of God is promised to be whatever we want it to be. There is no arbitrary assignment that takes place at the great "police court in the sky." Instead, the eternal invitation is offered: "Let him who desires take the water of life without price" (Revelation 22:17). Heaven is for those who want it, who love holiness, who like other people and want to love them. Hell is for those who love themselves exclusively and would shut others out. Whichever of these you choose, Jesus says of you, "they have their reward" (Matthew 6:16). But if you truly long for heaven, if it is that "sweet desire" for which all earthly desires are a distortion, which C. S. Lewis called

that unnameable something, desire for which pierces us like a rapier at the smell of a bonfire, the sound of wild ducks flying overhead, the title of *The Well at the World's End,* the opening lines of *Kubla Khan,* the morning cobwebs in late summer, or the noise of falling waves . . .[1]

then be sure you will find it. "He who seeks finds" (Luke 11:10).

On the other hand, if you despise love, and call it a weakness, like Nietzsche, or an opiate, like Marx . . . if you really hate God and all that he stands for, then no matter how sweet a draft is offered, you will find it bitter. Consider the unhappy dwarfs in Lewis's delightful children's tale:

Lucy led the way and soon they could all see the Dwarfs. They had a very odd look. They weren't strolling about or enjoying themselves (although the cords with which they had been tied seemed to have vanished) nor were they lying down and having a rest. They were sitting very close together in a little circle facing one another. They never looked round or took any notice of the humans till Lucy and Tirian were almost near enough to touch them. Then the Dwarfs all cocked their heads as if they couldn't see any one but were listening hard and trying to guess by the sound what was happening.

"Look out!" said one of them in a surly voice. "Mind where you're going. Don't walk into our faces!"

"All right!" said Eustace indignantly. "We're not blind. We've got eyes in our heads."

"They must be darn good ones if you can see in here," said the same Dwarf whose name was Diggle.

"In where?" asked Edmund.

"Why you bone-head, in *here* of course," said Diggle. "In this pitch-black, poky, smelly little hole of a stable."

"Are you blind?" said Tirian.

"Ain't we all blind in the dark!" said Diggle.

"But it isn't dark, you poor stupid Dwarfs," said Lucy. "Can't you see? Look up! Look round! Can't you see the sky and the trees and the flowers? Can't you see *me?*"

"How in the name of all Humbug can I see what ain't there? And how can I see you any more than you can see me in this pitch darkness?"

"But I *can* see you," said Lucy. "I'll prove I can see you. You've got a pipe in your mouth."

"Anyone that knows the smell of baccy could tell that," said Diggle.

"Oh the poor things! This is dreadful," said Lucy. Then she had an idea. She stooped and picked some wild violets. "Listen, Dwarf," she said. "Even if your eyes are wrong, perhaps your nose is all right: can you smell *that*." She leaned across and held the fresh, damp flowers to Diggle's ugly nose. But she had to jump back quickly in order to avoid a blow from his hard little fist.

"None of that!" he shouted. "How dare you! What do you mean by shoving a lot of filthy stable-litter in my face? There was a thistle in it too. It's like your sauce! And who are you anyway?"

"Earthman," said Tirian, "she is the Queen Lucy, sent hither by Aslan out of the deep past. And it is for her sake alone that I, Tirian, your lawful King, do not cut all your heads from your shoulders, proved and twice-proved traitors that you are."

"Well if that doesn't beat everything!" exclaimed Diggle. "How *can* you go on talking all that rot? Your wonderful Lion didn't come and help you, did he? Thought not. And now—even now—when you've been beaten and shoved into this black hole, just the same as the rest of us, you're still at your old game. Starting a new lie! Trying to make us believe we're none of us shut up, and it ain't dark, and heaven knows what."

"There *is* no black hole, save in your own fancy, fool," cried Tirian. "Come *out* of it." And, leaning forward, he caught Diggle by the belt and the hood and swung him right out of the circle of Dwarfs. But the moment Tirian put him down, Diggle darted back to his place among the others, rubbing his nose and howling:

"Ow! Ow! What d'you do that for! Banging my face against the wall. You've nearly broken my nose."

"Oh dear!" said Lucy. "What *are* we to do for them?"

"Let 'em alone," said Eustace: but as he spoke the earth trembled. The sweet air grew suddenly sweeter. A brightness flashed behind them. All turned. Tirian turned last because he was afraid. There stood his heart's desire, huge and real, the golden Lion, Aslan himself, and already the others were kneeling in a circle round his forepaws and burying their hands and faces in his mane as he stooped his great head to touch them with his tongue. Then he fixed his eyes upon Tirian, and Tirian came near, trembling, and flung himself at the Lion's feet, and the Lion kissed him and said, "Well done, last of the Kings of Narnia who stood firm at the darkest hour."

"Aslan," said Lucy through her tears, "could you—will you—do something for these poor Dwarfs?"

"Dearest," said Aslan, "I will show you both what I can, and what I cannot, do." He came close to the Dwarfs and gave a long growl: low, but it set all the air shaking. But the Dwarfs said to one another, "Hear that? That's the gang at the other end of the Stable. Trying to frighten us. They do it with a machine of some kind. Don't take any notice. They won't take *us* in again!"

Aslan raised his head and shook his mane. Instantly a glorious feast appeared on the Dwarfs' knees: pies and tongues and pigeons and trifles and ices, and each Dwarf had a goblet of good wine in his right hand. But it wasn't much use. They began eating and drinking greedily enough, but it was clear that they couldn't taste it properly. They thought they were eating and drinking only the sort of things you might find in a Stable. One said he was trying to eat hay and another said he had got a bit of an old turnip and a third said he'd found a raw cabbage leaf. And they raised golden goblets of rich red wine to their lips and said "Ugh! Fancy drinking dirty water out of a trough that a donkey's been at! Never thought we'd come to this." But very soon every Dwarf began suspecting that every other Dwarf had found something nicer than he had, and they started grabbing and snatching, and went on to quarrelling, till in a few minutes there was a free fight and all the good food was smeared on their faces and clothes or trodden under foot. But when at last they sat down to nurse their black eyes and their bleeding noses, they all said:

"Well, at any rate there's no Humbug here. We haven't let anyone take us in. The Dwarfs are for the Dwarfs."

"You see," said Aslan. "They will not let us help them. They have chosen cunning instead of belief. Their prison is only in their own minds, yet they are in that prison; and so afraid of being taken in that they can not be taken out." [2]

For Andy Capp the good is sometimes hard to see. His long-suffering, faithful wife is rarely seen as such. Usually when he thinks of marriage, it carries a terrible weight of chronic pain. Home is not security, it is prison; marriage is not companionship, it is bondage, even when considered in the abstract:

Andy has chosen his world, and elected to "sin boldly." If he were plunged into a society devoid of vice, he would be miserable. Even a hangover can come to be loved for the delicious sense of feeling sorry for oneself. There are those who, even if they cannot scratch, would rather itch than not. The proof of this in Andy is that you find him there. A quick survey of his adventures shows that they concern themselves mostly with the following matters, in order of their importance: the pain of being married (or separated), laziness, violence, drunkenness, sexual license, poverty, and gambling. If he doesn't like it, why does he

keep coming back? And if there isn't at least a surreptitious liking for it in each of us, why do we keep on reading about his exploits in the daily newspapers?

Let's face it. Our parents tried hard for us not to find it out, and we have tried hard not to admit it to ourselves or our children, but what we might call Capp's Law remains true as of old, namely:

Sin is fun.

There is no getting around it.

In certain moments, maudlin with the effects of booze, our hero knows the meaning of shame. His penitence is sincere, but its depth is doubtful.

He enjoys his sins, and he doesn't intend to change.

This does not mean, of course, that Andy doesn't know the difference between right and wrong. If that were so, he would be

a purely amoral being, like the beasts of the field, and his behavior excusable on that basis. But, more important, it wouldn't
be nearly as much fun. Stolen melons are sweeter. For sin to
amount to anything, it has to be deliberate. Accidents don't
count. (On this basis, the Fall of Man ought more properly to be
called the Jump or the Plunge.) Andy knows the difference. He
respects the right from a certain viewpoint (on one occasion he
embarrasses Flo in church by breaking into spontaneous applause
at a sermon of which he approves), and to a degree he lives
within its rules. But they are a structure *against* which he grinds
out his life-style. Within the framework of the laws of his community he shapes a pattern of joyful wickedness. The lines that
delineate his orbit are the hours of the opening and closing of the
pub, the necessity of putting in a token appearance at the em-
ployment exchange to keep his unemployment check coming, the
need to pacify his patient wife just enough to keep his meals coming and his clothes clean, the coming of the football season, and
the horrid inevitability of middle age. Within these limits he cuts a
clever and arrogant swath. His brushes with the law are rare, and
almost always end in his triumphant refusal to be intimidated by
the forces of righteousness.

He knows what right is, and to some degree he struggles to do it, but the struggle is doomed to failure. He fights to make the game interesting, as a porcupine is more interesting than a clam. But it is a losing battle. As Eliza Doolittle's father sings in *My Fair Lady,*

With a little bit of luck,
When temptation comes you'll give right in![3]

But no one ever sets out to be a "bad person." Can you imagine a young man setting his sights as he enters college to become the worst sort of fellow he can imagine? That may be his aim, but he will not be so honest as to call it that, even to himself. He will give it nicer-sounding names. He will aim for money, success, prestige, fulfillment, self-discovery, pleasure, or the like. You will never hear him call it greed, corruption, or wickedness. Even a Hitler shapes his conquests in the name of democracy or law and order. When Adam committed the first sin,* it was not a blatant attempt at evil. It was to eat of the fruit of the tree of knowledge, which the serpent promised him would make him like God! The first sin is in trying to be like God (or, if you like etymology, in trying to be good)!

Andy Capp does not set out to be "bad" as such; he sets out to "'ave a nice time," but the not-so-original sin is in him, and he is licked before he starts.

---

* Some biblical authorities will try to argue that it was Eve who did this first, but in the paternalistic world of Andy Capp such nonsense is unacceptable. Only a man could rise to such heights.

Thus Andy the sinner—a comfort to the three billion rest of us on the planet—consoles us with the reality known to every theologian worthy of the name:

Humanum est errare.

Now then, is it possible that Andy Capp has any good in him?

3.

Andy the Saint

Is there any good in Andy Capp? This is a vital issue, because, believe me, if there is good in him, then there is hope for the rest of us, for he is our ideal scoundrel. The title of this chapter is deliberately chosen to make a point—namely, that a good man is not necessarily a perfect man. The word "saint" is a New Testament word, and there it does *not* mean what it has come to mean in the vocabulary of modern man. Usually when today's folk speak of someone as a saint they mean that he is superhuman (that is, the right caliber to be put in the canon). You hear it in sentences like this: "I don't see why that trouble happened to Aunt Soso—why she was a saint if there ever was one."* But in the letters of the early church, the word simply means the members of the congregation, those who are communicants at a particular place, as in the letter of Paul which is addressed:

> To all the saints in Christ Jesus who are at Philippi, with the bishops and deacons. [Philippians 1:1]

The word means literally "those sanctified, or set apart for God." It is God who is good and righteous altogether, not man. God gives man whatever goodness he has.† Therefore a church member

---

* By the way, the answer to this particular question is found in the Sermon on the Mount, Matthew 5:45.

† The world believes that God runs a school and grades everybody from A to F, those who pass being given admission to heaven. No way. The Bible teaches that God gives everybody an A if they want it, but lots of folks would rather flunk than take charity. (See Ephesians 2:8.)

(as Andy Capp) is not necessarily a better person than a non-churchman. He may even be much worse. It is not his goodness but his *chosen*-ness that makes him a part of the kingdom.

So Andy Capp is not perfect. But we still are asking our question: Is there any good in him at all?

Well, there are several things we can say in his favor. Starting with the least sophisticated virtues, one thing you can certainly affirm about Andy is his powerful capacity to win. He has been known to lose, but almost never in physical combat.

The respect he wins among his male peers for this is something barely short of wonderful. The girls like it in him, too, but there is something about this feisty, scrappy little man that makes every male who dreams of glory take heart. He is defender of the home, liberty, and the right to be myself. However vicious he may appear to the world's pacifists, to the chauvinist in the average human male he is something of a hero. Even the people he destroys in battle love him. They respect him, for they too are fighters, and they love a champion. To be beaten by him is to delight in him. There seems to be a masochistic streak in the male.

But let's move beyond merely physical aggressiveness. We have already used the phrase "sin boldly" as it applies to Andy. It was originally used by Martin Luther in a letter to Philip Melanchthon in August of 1851.* Of course, it is a dangerous phrase, for it can either mean utter selfishness or be a form of humility. But who is the more selfish (or at least self-conscious) —the man who goes ahead and does it with gusto, or the man who spends hours weighing the consequences, wondering what his conscience will say, what God and his neighbors will think, and what the outcome will be? There is an arrogance in Andy Capp that sets him free from ordinary egotism into a world of grace that few mortals can know.

* Luther also added, "But trust God even more boldly." We'll have to talk about Andy Capp's faith before we are through.

But how can a committed man of faith condone such behavior? If Luther was really a reformer, how did he dare counsel
sin? It's not that Luther was in favor of sin, it is that he was willing to face *reality*. I *am* a sinner—there is no getting around
that—so I might as well relax and enjoy it.

Andy Capp goes through life almost oblivious of the contradiction between his healthy opinion of himself and his unhealthy attitude toward others. Notice in the preceding cartoon strip how blithely he sings of benevolence toward the human race, and how swiftly he switches gears. He *really* believes in himself. With one notable omission he fits C. S. Lewis's description:

> Do not imagine that if you meet a really humble man he will be what most people call "humble" nowadays: he will not be a sort of greasy, smarmy person, who is always telling you that, of course, he is nobody. Probably all you will think about him is that he seemed a cheerful, intelligent chap who took a real interest in what *you* said to *him*. If you do dislike him it will be because you feel a little envious of anyone who seems to enjoy life so easily.[1]

If you omit the middle sentence, you have a perfect description of Andy Capp! He may not be a humble man, but there is something about him that is very closely kin to humility. What is it?

The clue to Andy Capp is his *honesty*. Not that he has never been known to tell a lie (on the contrary, he is an artist at convincing his wife that he has caught a fish, or won at the races, or not been misbehaving), but that he is at heart an honest man.

Honesty and humility are related. It is almost impossible for any of us to be very objective about ourselves; we are invariably giving ourselves the benefit of the doubt, even when there isn't any. We find that Paul's dictum is impossible to obey:

> I bid every one among you not to think of himself more highly than he ought to think, but to think with sober judgment, each according to the measure of faith which God has assigned him. [Romans 12:3]

We cannot, as Robert Burns warned, achieve the power "to see oursels as ithers see us!" We have our own red-letter edition of the evidence: what appeals to us and supports our prejudices we see standing out; what bothers us we overlook. (This even includes the so-called "inferiority complex." Such a person is not truly humble; he is merely preoccupied with himself in a different way.)

If we were honest, would we not be more humble? That is, we would be aware of our faults, and not so shy about using our talents and our strengths. (Maybe that soprano singing so loudly in church is not trying to call attention to herself; possibly she is simply free enough to rejoice in a talent God has given her without worrying over whether anyone will notice or not.) So Andy Capp asserts himself—rudely, bluntly, but with a kind of honesty you can't help admiring.

If you confronted Andy with this chapter, I doubt if you would get much satisfaction out of him. He is not given to introspection anyway, but even if he were, I doubt if he believes himself to be particularly honest. That is because the culture in which he has developed has taught him that honesty lies primarily in the realm of prohibitions: Thou shalt not steal; thou shalt not bear false witness. And Andy is aware of the fact that he does these things. But it is his honesty that makes him aware of his dishonesty. So he might tell you that he is a liar, if you asked him outright, but he would tell you that because he is honest.*

When he sets out to attempt overt honesty, it fails him:

_____

* Please do not re-read this paragraph. I had enough trouble not re-writing it.

Or does it? Which is better, to maintain the secret sin which festers and infects the relationship, or to bring it out, face the pain of battle, and have it done with? There are times when open confrontation with hostility is far more useful than grumbling politeness. For Andy Capp there is usually no choice, for he will be himself. Indeed, he believes in himself.

The word "grace" is about as misused and misunderstood as any religious term, in spite of its popularity. We know that grace is "Amazing," or that it should be said before meals, or

that ballerinas have it, but we don't know what it means. In the New Testament "grace" translates the word from which we get the English word "charity," that which is given to the undeserving. In the Old Testament, it is kin to the Hebrew word that is translated "mercy" or "loving-kindness." It is a word rich with release: the dancer leaps with grace because she is released from the woodenness that imprisons the rest of us; we say it before meals because we are released from starvation; we sing that it is amazing because "'twas grace my fears relieved," and by some astonishing miracle, I know that the universe affirms my being. God loves me, even though my middle name is Andy Capp.

When I begin to know the meaning of grace in my own life, I begin to live with a new kind of freedom—almost an abandon. Andy Capp is on the verge of discovering this. And thus he believes in himself. He has a happy arrogance, which may be essentially selfish, but which is close to that genuine liberation that is born of true faith in the forgiveness of God.

It never occurs to him (sober) to question his innocence. He has heard the commandment "you shall love your neighbor as yourself," and he is perfecting the self-love that it specifies. He is a thoroughly selfish man, and thus he breaks through the bottom of selfishness and out into a new level of humility.

There is a form of arrogance that is hard to distinguish from humility. It is depicted by Howard Roark, Ayn Rand's intractable

architect in *The Fountainhead*. He is so obsessed with himself
that he does not give a damn about the "things" that selfish men
customarily gather around them. Money, prestige, power—none
of them matter. There is only one thing he wants, he says to a
prospective client:

> My work done my way. . . . there's nothing in the world that you
> can offer me, except this. Offer me this and you can have any-
> thing I've got to give. My work done my way. A private, personal,
> selfish, egotistical motivation. That's the only way I function. That's
> all I am.[2]

He is, as he asserts, a selfish man. And yet there is a certain noble
disregard of custom and pretense in his arrogance that makes him
a sympathetic character. And that is the humility of Andy Capp.
He is simply too selfish to believe that he needs to defend his
honor or his pride, and so he assumes that he is worthy.

Now it is obvious on the face of it that Andy Capp is almost exactly the opposite of what we mean when we speak of a person who lives "under grace." And yet we are hard pressed to explain just what the difference is. As an extreme rightist and an extreme leftist often meet each other backing around the world, so the saint and the sinner have more in common than first meets the eye. Perhaps this is why, when the most saintly man ever known came along, he was found more often in the company of disreputable characters, accused by the more traditional religious community of drunkenness, carousing, and consorting with criminals.

Good or bad, there are few men who can attack life with genuine joy, live it for its own sake, and come off a winner:

There are psychologists who argue that if the church would say less about sin, people who are now so preoccupied with guilt would begin naturally to live creative lives. Then there are theologians who argue that if the psychologists would say less about neurosis, people who are so preoccupied with their own peculiarities would forget them and begin naturally to live creative lives.

There is Andy, philosophically and theologically, crying both to God and to man, "Leave me alone! Let me survive in the least noticeable kind of way. I don't ask to be famous. Don't try to sell me a Calvinist work-ethic. Don't expect me to be an evangelist or a change-agent or anything else that is my neighbor's. Just leave me alone!"

He has a point. For every flag-waving, cause-championing reformer there needs to be a voice speaking out on behalf of life here and now. You can't spend all your energy struggling to graduate; you have to live in relationship to the other sophomores around you. Life was not meant for *whenever* and *if*, but for *meanwhile back at the ranch.* Not that progress isn't good and reform often necessary, but that most of the time what we need to do with the air is breathe it.

There is a kind of celebration about Andy, a sacramental view of life, that views it as a gift, not to be tampered with. "Begone!" he cries, to the social director, the priest, the policeman, the politician, the administrator, the committee chairman, the superintendent, the choir director, the polltaker, the behavioral scientist, and the tent preacher.

And off he goes, a thoroughly selfish man, thoroughly self-satisfied.

How does he get away with it? Is there any hope that I could live like that too? And if not, why not? What, in the long run, is wrong with selfishness as a way of life?

Well, for one thing . . .

4.
The Death of Joy

For one thing, when thoroughgoing selfishness becomes a way of life, joy begins to die, little by little. If I take myself too seriously I very soon find that my petty peeves become major issues, and my cynicism a world view. Selfishness looks like joy at first, but in the long run it is a cruel god, destroying those who worship it. It is like the little train in the parable that decided to jump the track and go wherever it wanted to. For a moment it was free, but then it got mired down in a cornfield and became immobile. Freedom, or at least joy, depends to some extent on staying on the track.

To some, freedom means the same thing as being broke. So long as I have my self-respect, my money, my country, my family, and my church demanding that I protect, support, and perhaps worship them, then I am not free. In that sense I am bound by the things that are important to me. Most people accept this slavery regularly. As one anti-women's-libber put it, "I'm proud of being a housewife. It makes me feel feminine, wanted, needed, and useful. I'm glad to give of myself for my husband and my children." This viewpoint is often expressed:

Freedom demands responsibility.

It depends, then, on what you mean by freedom. The freedom that Andy Capp has is not always as nice as it looks from this side of the fence. True, he is free from labor, discipline, responsibility, and duty, but he is a slave to his own self-regard. As a result he takes himself far too seriously, and is not free to enjoy or appreciate the world. Its splendor leaves him cold, for somehow something of the joy within him is beginning to die.

Like all Celts, and for the same reason, Andy cannot handle emotions in himself. He detests them. They frighten him. He is afraid that if he lets himself feel, he will be hurt.* Like the Scots of Drumtochty, he has emotions, but he dares not admit them:

---

* Which, of course, he will be; but those who are never hurt are dead.

Had any native used "magnificent," there would have been an uneasy feeling in the Glen; the man must be suffering from wind in the head, and might upset the rotation of crops, sowing his young grass after potatoes, or replacing turnip with beetroot. But nothing of that sort happened in my time; we kept ourselves well in hand. It rained in torrents elsewhere, with us it only "threatened tae be weet"—some provision had to be made for the deluge. Strangers, in the pride of health, described themselves as "fit for anything," but Hillocks, who died at ninety-two, and never had an hour's illness, did not venture, in his prime, beyond "Gaein' aboot, a'm thankfu' to say, gaein' aboot."

When one was seriously ill, he was said to be "gey an' sober," and no one died in Drumtochty—"he slippit awa."

Hell and heaven were pulpit words; in private life we spoke of "the ill place" and "oor lang hame."

When the corn sprouted in the stooks one late wet harvest, and Burnbrae lost half his capital, he only said, "It's no lichtsome," and no congratulations on a good harvest ever extracted more from Drumsheugh than "A' daurna complain." [1]

Granted, the dour Scottish talk leaves room for the deluge, but it also establishes a pattern of dishonesty that is implanted in generations to come. The fathers eat the sour grapes, and the children's teeth are set on edge (Jeremiah 31:29; Ezekiel 18:2). There are in America today children of Scots who came over with Flora MacDonald, *before the Revolutionary War,* who cannot embrace their sons or speak lovingly to their wives. There is something to be said for the Latin temperament. Better to be cursed by the father who can also express his love in no uncertain terms than to be ignored by the parent who can be neither angry nor glad.*

In Andy Capp's case, he cannot allow himself affection.

---

* It is very important that the reader understand this is no pejorative attack on Scots' reticence. Reticence is a virtue (at least in the first generation), and to be venerated. But when it becomes (as it often does in succeeding years) a denial of feeling altogether, it is a violation of the biblical instructions we have to let our emotions hang out. For example, no orthodox Highland Scot could ever be obedient to Paul's command "Be angry" in Ephesians 4:26. He is too busy worrying about having emotions at all to concern himself with the time limit (sundown).

He can express himself on the football field (where emotion is permissible),* but he cannot allow his wife to kiss him in public—it would be too embarrassing.

There is a sense in which joy eludes him at every point. The man who finds joy in false gods becomes a slave to them, and cannot touch the true God when he sees him. Whenever "sex" becomes a substitute for love, love becomes impossible. So, Andy Capp, searching (like all of us) for happiness, loses it at the last, out of the very intensity of his own searching (Luke 9:24).

There comes at last to the cynic a kind of deadly atmosphere which affects all around him; he for whom joy has died begins to will it dead for everybody else.

It's a dangerous game to play. The first time you hear a grouchy clergyman say, "Morning prayers! Why, I don't even believe in God until after my ten-o'clock coffee!" it is fairly funny, but after a few years it begins to grow cobwebs and smell of old attics. Poor old Andy Capp . . . the child in him is dying. It is harder and harder for him to be naive about anything, or to laugh at himself.

And that's really too bad, for there is so much in him that is delightful. He tries so hard not to be middle-aged. If only he could learn to accept an occasional touch of rheumatism with a grin (however wry) and to rejoice in what Reuel Howe calls "the creative years." If only he could be amused (however mildly) at his hunger for love, and his flight into alcohol and violence as substitutes, a kind of richness might pervade his life. But no, he will not look at the truth about himself, and when it finally forces its way into his consciousness it hurts more than he can bear.

---

* I have attended football games which were religious experiences, including such details as the prayer of invocation, the singing of hymns, and the taking of offerings. If some of *that* emotion could spill over into church on Sunday the kingdom might come. (Do you want it to?)

Once he asks a young chick, "Where 'ave you been all my life?" and she replies:

And the gloom settles in upon him, the deadly ennui that envelopes all who fear to taste reality. Life is never nothing. Only death is nothing (and for that reason to be dreaded both more and less than it is). Life is always something. But to the one who wishes he were someone else (a rich man, or a young man, or a good man), it feels empty.

Sic transit Andy Capp, missing out on the goodies of the world as he goes, his manic-depressive cycle alternating between ferocity and fear, bliss and boredom. There are better ways to exist. But before you pat yourself on the back and decide that you're a better man than 'e is, take a hard look at your own comings and goings. How free are you from the deadly mist? Be careful how you give him advice.

5.

Cherchez la Femme

There is one person who is really qualified to give Andy advice, but she happens to be the one to whom he is least likely to listen. At first glance, Florrie Capp appears to be the least liberated woman in captivity, leading a life of sheer drudgery in bondage to the world's champion lout.

But is she? There is about her a certain native shrewdness that forces you from wonder to admiration. Unquestionably she emerges as the stronger of the two. Is she there because she has to be, or because she wants to? She has left him as many times as he has left her, but she always comes back. You can understand why Andy comes back—security, affection, to have his socks darned . . . But what could possibly keep Flo returning to the salt mines?

For one thing, it isn't always as bad as it appears on the surface. As an oyster learns to cover the grit that irritates and so builds a pearl, so, it seems, a versatile human being can get used to anything, maybe even like it. There are compensations in living with a man like Andy, especially if you can outwit him.

And generally she does. Although her antagonist is formidable (having practically invented the excuse and the lie), she has created her own private system of survival. It may not be ideal, it may even be highly unpleasant at times, but the fact remains that it works, it enables her to cope. And that is more than can be said for many systems.

Who knows where she will come out? Flo is forever perfecting the pearl, coating it with layer upon layer of her own particular brand of loving deceit, calculated to make a man out of her man. She is playing with dynamite—he does not like to be tampered with. But it seems that dynamite is more fun to play with than stovewood.*

---

* My mother never warned me not to play with stovewood—not because it wasn't dangerous but because it wasn't interesting.

No, she never gives up. In spite of the pain,* she dusts herself off and comes back for more. It is a refreshing affirmation of life, and a kind of bloody-but-unbowed acceptance of the inevitable. If Andy sins boldly, Flo lives boldly. She is a Dionysian, a celebrationist, a believer in hidden grace. It does not surprise her that life is full of pain—nobody ever promised her a rose garden. The rose is inside of her, and she brings it to bloom in her courageous will to live.†

While Andy flees from reality, Florrie attacks it. She is a realist, a pessimist, a cynic, and a skeptic; ‡ she expects to be shot down, but she keeps on coming. Andy is busy turning his feelings off, and so joy for him is dying. Flo would rather hurt than have

---

* Although it isn't as easy to spot, it is the heart's pain, not the physical pain, that really hurts Flo. She is one tough knot!

† Not that Flo isn't sometimes an escapist, but as somebody has said, escapism is not a bad word if you are in jail.

‡ All of these can be good words if you come at them from the blind side.

no feelings at all. So she rolls up her sleeves and wades in, determined to live and love in the world as it is. She neither asks why the universe is as it is, nor frets because it is not as she would will it. She is like the not-so-dumb girl who responded as follows when her date started blowing his philosophical horn:

HE: You know, the universe is a strange and marvelous place!

SHE: Compared to what?

How does one go about living creatively in a miserable situation? Is it simply a matter of "singing hymns in prison," with a kind of bland disregard of the ugly facts? Not for Flo! She comes at it with a shrewd and mischievous ability to pick through the rubbish of her man and discover something of value there after all. It doesn't take much:

"Looking on the bright side" is as old as Aesop,* and it doesn't take much wisdom to discover it in principle, but putting it to work requires a devious mind. You have to be alert for the slightest shade of difference:

PESSIMIST: My cup is half empty.

OPTIMIST: My cup is half full!

Out of the ashes of discouragement, given the will to see it, rises a phoenix of hope.

Is this simply, in another guise, the "power of positive thinking"? Not for Florrie. She is as negative as they come. Every ounce of her being calls forth cynicism . . . and it is in the midst of that negative that her positive is discovered. It is, if we can approach holy places without stumbling into blasphemy, passing through Calvary to get to Easter morning. Florrie suffers the pain of reality, and gathering it to her bosom, she takes her stand.

---

* Around 550 B.C. he said, "There is always someone worse off than yourself." Can you think of any earlier optimism?

Observe that, as in the cartoon strip above, there is a strange violation of logic in this capacity to love the unlovable. It violates all the laws of common sense, as much as Jesus' absurd advice that whoever would find his life must lose it. But the foolishness of God is wiser than men. And when you take it out in the sunlight, it has to make you laugh (if you're not crying). I once overheard two little-league baseball coaches in a screaming argument over a contested play at home plate. Finally, as the insults reached their apex, one of them announced: "All right, Charlie, you know what you are!" To which Charlie replied, without a moment's hesitation, "Nobody can call me that and get away with it!" When the laughter had subsided, the fight was over.

Down the road goes Florrie, staring the bitter truth in the face, and grumbling under her breath at the blow she has been dealt by life. But as she goes, the grumble works its way into a grin, and the grin into rejoicing. A Dionysian gladness replaces the anger, and all is well. Can it be that, as May Wynn said to Willie Keith, "Happy is when you don't have a broken leg," [1] or is it possible to discover some genuine delight in the midst of it all? Florrie Capp seems to combine a basic attitude of "don't cry over spilled milk" with an authentic Epicureanism. If she had read Lucretius she might say to herself:

Take hence thy tears, thou fool, thy whinings cease.
Filled with life's every blessing thou dost sink
Into thy grave; but since thou gapest e'er
For what thou lackst, and scornest what is thine,
Joyless and unfulfilled thy life hath slipt
From out thy grasp.[2]

Instead, she breaks into song, piercing the gloom of her loneliness with a ray of hope.

The result of this astonishing turn, that is, joy in the midst of adversity, is a miracle. Not only does she love life in spite of its pain, but *the very pain itself becomes a blessing.* It is something like the comfort that the bottle gives an alcoholic who despises it . . . something like the beauty that comes at last to the face of an ugly mate of many years . . . something like the security of the fleshpots of Egypt . . . but perhaps more than any of these, it is like the love of battle which comes to a soldier.

The appearance of the atoll was not yet marred by the attack. The orange billows of flame here and there were decorative touches to the pleasant verdant islands, and so were the freshly blossoming clouds of black and white smoke. The smell of powder drifted in the air, and, for Willie, somehow completed the festive and gay effect of the morning. He could not have said why. Actually, it was because the odor, with the incessant banging, reminded him of fireworks on the Fourth of July.[3]

And so, even when she has been granted shore leave . . . when it would be possible to forsake it all, the pain and the put-downs, forever . . . she returns to the battle.

O Wonder! She is in love.

6.

He Loves Her, Too

This is a short chapter, because it is a lot easier to explain why Andy loves Flo. He's got a good thing going. She relates to him with a kind of grace that makes his useless way of life possible. She labors for him, cooks, darns, blesses, and forgives him. But best of all, she lets him be himself. She turns him loose, as the Waiting Father sent forth his Prodigal Son, to go to hell if he insisted on it. She acts as one who believes that "Love is a spendthrift, leaves its arithmetic at home, is always 'in the red.' " [1]

Not that Flo is completely permissive. On the contrary, the relationship is a highly complicated one. As Thomas Harris has reminded us,

> The relationship of many couples is a complicated mesh of games, wherein accumulated resentment and bitterness have produced intricate, repeated versions of "Uproar," "It's All You," "Blemish," "So's Your Old Man," and "If It Weren't for You I Could." The rules and stereotyped plays in these games are catalogued in great detail in Berne's *Games People Play*, which has been one of the standard manuals assigned for reading to couples in treatment. These games all grow from the early childhood game of "Mine Is Better," designed to overcome the original fear of being

cheated. One of the most brilliant exposés of a game existence is written by Edward Albee in the already-mentioned *Who's Afraid of Virginia Wolf?* This play illustrates that despite all the desperation produced, there still are enough secondary benefits that the games, in a sense, hold the marriage together.[2]

Thus Florrie wastes her love as far as she can stand to do it, till her own need takes over, and she draws the line where she must.

So it is no wonder that Andy loves Flo! She achieves, through games and grace, a delicate balance that keeps him moving. He is permitted to indulge his laziness, his drunkenness, and his middle-aged romantic notions enough to satisfy the itch, but he is pestered regularly into applying for work, attempting something around the house, or otherwise moving a little so that he does not rust permanently in the same position. Through devious means she protects him from himself, at the same time she permits him to be himself.

If you asked Andy why he loves Florrie, I doubt if he could tell you. I'm not even sure he knows that he does—he doesn't say so very often. But occasionally, born perhaps out of the dim memory of a romantic youth, the delicious truth arises in him: This is his kind of woman!

What draws two people together? If the notion that marriages are made in heaven has any validity, then the marriage of Flo and Andy must call the Divine Wisdom into question.* They might feel like saying, as the temperance lecturer did when reminded that Jesus had turned water into wine, "I know it, and I'd of thought a lot better of him if he hadn't of done it!" People get married because:

( ) they are rebounding
( ) they need to get out of a bad home
( ) they feel a physical "thing" for each other
( ) there isn't anybody else (they think)
( ) they both like horses or something
( ) none of the above

They just do it! By the thousands daily, couples march to altars and arbors, and marry for love or money or whatever. But they do not know what they are getting into! It takes a decade, a lifetime, to discover the truth, and by then, even the faults of a mate have become so much a part of your life that you miss them when he's gone.

Maybe the angels know something. It seems that they have given up marriage, in favor, no doubt, of an even deeper system of relationships that we are not capable of. (See Matthew 24:38.) But on this side of the Jordan, human ties, even the best of them, have their lumps. And who would give it up? Bad as it is, this is reality. And the very act of taking marriage vows gives a possessiveness to the relationship that makes it brighter. With apologies to Proverbs 21:9:

It is better to live with a contentious woman than all by yourself in a corner.

It is like the old political tale. The veteran Democrat is chastized

---

* We have already had something to say about the foolishness of God. (See 1 Corinthians 1:25.) If we're going to start criticizing the way he runs things, why stop with Andy Capp's marriage? How do you like the way the human race is arranged?

for supporting McGovern and Shriver in 1972. "Don't you know
they are radical leftists?" he is asked. "Maybe so," he replies,
"but they're *our* radical leftists."

So, if you want to test Andy's affection for Flo, criticize her
in front of him, but be prepared to duck.

7.
What's the Use?

So we have established, tentatively and tenuously, that they love each other. So what? What sort of existence is it which finds first one and then the other of the participants battered about the head and shoulders, physically if not mentally?* Why do they keep coming back for more? Surely there is something other than

---

* To those who glibly claim that spiritual suffering is much worse than physical, I offer the sage advice of Charlie Brown: "Pain *hurts*!"

heroic nihilism operative here! Can this be all there is to reality? Why don't they leave each other? What sort of masochism keeps a wife forever nursing back to sobriety an alcoholic husband? Or, on a slightly higher plane, how do you account for the woman who keeps eternal vigil beside the bed of a comatose husband, spoon-feeding and talking baby talk although no response whatever comes from the sick man? In such situations, as in that of Andy and Flo, it is obvious to ask, "What keeps them going?"

Perhaps it is not so obvious, but equally important, to ask what keeps the best of marriages going? Are there really saints who honestly claim that "never has a cross word or an angry gesture passed between us"? Whenever anyone makes such a claim, the cynic in me always mutters under his breath, "Well then, I bet they have never communicated with each other at all!" Anger is a part of life, and is present in every human relationship. Inhabitants of Mediterranean countries have known this for centuries, and have learned the place of a little healthy scream-

ing and hollering, but the Saxon folk still restrain their emotions with a skill little short of astonishing. (See pages 55–56, especially footnotes.) The result of this "covered fury" may be perforated ulcers or periodic depressions, but in any case it does not succeed in doing away with the anger. Even in the best of relationships, anger is there. There never was man or woman saintly enough that you could be married to them without getting angry at some point. And even if there were, *that* would be grounds for fury indeed. Sooner or later you would have to scream out, "Do you have to be so all-fired perfect? Couldn't you make at least *one* mistake as a sign of your humanity?"

Humanity! That's the rub! It is the nature of the human beast to be untrustworthy, disloyal, unhelpful, unfriendly, discourteous, unkind, disobedient, grouchy, profligate, cowardly, dirty, and irreverent: "a fiend to all, and a bother to every other Scout." Why should you stay married to one of them? Why not take a trip to the South Seas? Or become a rich playboy? Or a poor playboy? Or anything other than a poor beastie, caught in the trap of an unpleasant relationship, whether it is your fault or the other's? What is the point of saving a marriage?

Andy does not know the answer to that question, because it is based on a false premise. It is predicated on the notion that preserving a marriage is a rational thing to do. But it isn't . . . it's an act of faith. Webster defines a person as one who thinks, feels, and wills. *Thinking* is rational, *feeling* is emotional, but *willing* is something more than the other two put together. It is the act of a whole being, an integrated self, which makes moral choice not simply on the basis of brain or viscera, but out of the miracle of faith. That is the difference between man and beast.

The code of the animal is: *If it feels good, do it!*
The code of the computer is: *If it makes sense, do it!*
But the code of a man is: *Do it if you must!**

No man stays with his wife because she is better looking than Marilyn Monroe (not even *her* husbands stayed with her), and

---

* I don't care if you think I mean that he is predestined to do it, or that he wills to do it. For the life of me, I can't see the difference between having to because God makes me, or having to because my being decides it. If you have to, you have to.

no man stays with his wife for sound business reasons. In the same way, no man believes in God because he can prove it, or because it comforts him: the atheist has just as many intellectual proofs as the Christian (more, because it's important to him), and the idea of God can be just as terrifying as it is comforting.* Marriage, like belief in God, is an act of faith, and therefore it is a gift.

Does it feel good to Andy that he is married to Flo? No.

---

* Have you ever wondered why, in the Bible, every time an angel appears, the first thing he has to say is "Fear not"?

"It's not that I don't love yer, Florrie. It's just that the idea of a second honeymoon sickens me."

Does it make *sense* to Andy that he is married to Flo? No.

Nor does it feel good or make sense to Flo to be married to Andy. They are together because they have to be.

What then? Is the universe insane? Are we all mad, "Lost and hopeless and condemned on this rock that goes 'round the sun without meaning"? [1] No, there is a deeper reason, deeper than human reason and deeper than human emotion. It transcends them both, and it is at the heart of the universe. It is the absurd divinity that caused Christ to empty himself of his equality with God (Philippians 2:5–11), and brought him at last to cry, "O God, where have you gone?" (Mark 15:34).

It is the unbelievable, liberating gospel that it is not approval, but acceptance, that redeems; not law, but grace—grace, that unmerited free gift, which makes possible not only marriage, but all human relationships, and in the end, salvation itself. All human relationships exist because sinful (lonely) people need each other. And so it is with Andy and Flo. In spite of all the powder and shot, when the smoke clears, it is better to have been in battle than to have had no relationship at all.

8.

They Need Each Other!

They need each other! "People who need people are the luckiest people in the world." [1] If that maxim holds water, then Andy and Flo must be luckier still. As sweet as the single life looks from this side of the fence, it has one ugly word that shatters all its glamour. And the word is *loneliness*.

Not that marriage per se is a cure for loneliness; on the contrary, it may be the cause of some of the emptiest feelings possible. But at least it provides a framework for attacking the problem, whereas singlehood demands that every relation be superficial to some degree. The trouble with being a priest is not the vows of celibacy (anybody can grit his teeth and abstain with pains); it's coming home to an empty rectory.

There are gregarious, well-loved people outside of marriage, and there are desperate, misanthropic people within it. But, other things being equal,* it is better to have loved and lost than never to have loved at all.

For one thing, marriage, like other institutions, provides a framework of hope.

> By His apostles, He has instructed those who enter into this relation to cherish a mutual esteem and love; to bear with each other's infirmities and weaknesses; to comfort each other in sickness, trouble, and sorrow; in honesty and industry to provide for each other . . . and to live together as heirs of the grace of life.[2]

---

* They aren't, of course.

The framework of grace—not to be confused with the ideals spelled out in the wedding vows (for which we aim, but which we never reach)—is that system of well-remembered ground rules and gamesmanship with which we come to be comforted and within which we can operate reasonably well. For example, if a man knows that certain phrases will make his wife furious, he is able to govern his destiny by avoiding them when he wants peace and quiet, and using them when he wants action.* In short, it doesn't matter too much which side the knife and fork are on at the table, as long as everybody knows where they are and can get

on with the business of eating. A marriage provides the table manners that free us to live.

If it weren't for this structure, however awkward and artificial, we would never be sure of ourselves at all, and constantly stumbling into folly. Think back to the first time you ever went

---

* Sometimes, of course, he may use the phrase without thinking, in which case he should say, "I'm sorry," unless *that* is a phrase which makes his wife furious, which it often is, depending on how you say it.

to a high school dance. Unless you want all through life to possess the same horrible feelings of "what do I say, what do I do?" that mark you as a newcomer, then some familiar structures are necessary. How if you had to learn every day what to do with everyone you met?

Or, as Tevye says, "Without our traditions, our lives would be as shaky as—as a fiddler on the roof!"

But beyond all this, it is the very agony of our sharp edges that gives us comfort.

Our disagreements are the grindstones against which we sharpen our self-understanding. How could children ever learn anything if life at home did not involve occasional burns, spills, embarrassments, tantrums, and the like? If it were not for the north wind, roots would never grow deep.* Those who live all their lives in sweetness and light never really live: they are like the man who fell into the vat of lanolin.† Of course, nobody is going to seek out poverty just because it may produce some vir-

---

* There are those who say that if it were not for the north wind roots would not *have* to grow deep, but there is a ready rejoinder to such a position. It is, "Shut up!"

† He softened to death.

tues, or deliberately chose bad-tasting medicine over good, as though the badness were *itself* a virtue. That would be a sin against the Holy Spirit, that is, to call good evil, and evil good, and it cannot be forgiven.* But it is hard exercise that produces trim bodies, and sweat that exudes excellence. Thus, caring quite often wears a mailed fist.

---

* For further research on this point, read Matthew, chapter 12. Of course the key verses are 31–32, but they must be seen in the light of the whole context. It is not that God's forgiveness isn't available to all; it is that the Pharisee in us will not admit that we need it. You can't forgive a man who doesn't know he is guilty. Or, as we have made the point earlier, if a man insists on going to hell, or wasting his substance in riotous living, or both, the door is always open.

Andy and Flo are so important to each other that if anything happened to either one of them it would be a shattering blow to the other. Most of the time grief comes harder to those who have hated their mates than to those who have lived happily ever after. When it has all been a teamwork, then death itself can be faced with equanimity, but when you have constantly screamed and nagged at each other, a huge void is left. As Queen Victoria said after the death of Albert, "Now there's no one left to call me @#&$¢#!" It's a lot quieter around the house when a barking dog is gone than it is when the cat ceases to sleep by the fire.

They need each other! They may not say it, but they do.

When all is said and done, the chauvinist who wrote

Women, women, women!
What can you do about 'em?
You can't get along with 'em,
And you can't get along without 'em!

knew whereof he spoke. Marriage may not be any fun, but it is certainly necessary.

And occasionally, by all that is holy, it *is* fun. Indeed, such fun as emerges, timid and peeking, from the caldron of a boiling, living, writhing, painful, human institution like marriage is just about the most fun there is.

9.
Facing Reality

So we come at last to the question of chapter one: When you peel the human creature down to his fundamental layer, is the thing you find there good or bad? And the answer, of course, is *yes*.

The fundamental anthropological question is "What of man?" and the answer is, he's human. This means two things, and a life lived without both of them is like a man with one shoe nailed to the floor—he goes in circles a lot. The two things are these:

1. Man is created in the image of God.
2. He has forgotten it.

If he remembered his divinity he would not need to create artificial positions of divinity by which he clobbers his neighbor. But he has forgotten it, so he creates them. The following is only a partial list of false gods, but it will serve to introduce us to the subject:

LUKMANOHANS,* the god of all show-offs. (Most often seen going before falls.)

MAMMON, the god of worldly possessions. (Has many temples downtown, some with Greek columns, some made of glass, but the principle is the same. So is the interest.)

---

* Pronounced like "Look, Ma, no hands!"

APHRODITE, the goddess of worldly pleasures. (Sometimes called simply "sex," which is misleading, since sex by itself is neither divine nor devilish. It's sort of like turkey hash— it depends on what you put in it and how it's served.)

HARVEY WALLBANGER, the god of escapism. (Sometimes called Morpheus, or Tom Collins, or occasionally Grass.)

PATRIA, the god of the "in" group, of race, or nation, or religion, or whatever, so long as it keeps somebody on the outside looking in.

And several others.

There would be no need to worship these false gods if we were only open to the presence of God himself within us. But we cannot be. We are blinded by a willful ignorance, built up over the centuries in the guise of human accomplishment, parental wisdom, the quest for success, happiness, fulfillment, and the *élan vital.* We like to think of the evolutionary process gradually opening up, like the chambered nautilus, till it achieves ultimate freedom. But what we seem to achieve is ultimate disintegration, Nirvana, a kind of nothing, because we were not meant to evolve into supermen; we were created in God's image, and that ought to be enough.

Jesus knew that it was enough. When the same temptation befell him that had come to the first Adam ("You shall be as God, able to turn stones into bread, to have angels catch you, to rule all the kingdoms of the world"), he did not fall for it, because he already knew who he was. He had heard the voice from heaven say to him, "You are my Son" (Luke 3:22), and he had nothing to prove. He was thus able to go about his work without defensiveness or pushiness. Often when he performed a miracle he would urge those he had helped to "tell no man" about the mysterious benefactor. Instead of calling himself divine, he preferred the title "the Son of Man," and he walked not with the religious set, but with the tax collectors and the streetwalkers. He could manage this life-style not because he was so "humble" (see the quote from C. S. Lewis on page 38), but because he knew his own strength. And he could pass this teaching on to his followers: "Happy are the meek, the poor in spirit, the mourners"—because their strength is not dependent on their own horn-blowing. As is written in the prophet Hezekiah, "He who hath the clout doth not need to shout."*

But, except for Jesus, the human race has failed the test. We want to be good, so we try so hard to do it that we fail . . . when all the time if we could only rely on the strength that is already there, it would be a snap. The best illustration is that of a child learning to swim. The instructor says, "The water will support you; just relax." But the child thinks, "What? That skinny stuff can't support me!" So he struggles and thrashes and gets water up his nose and has to be hauled out. "You see!" he rages, "I told you that it wouldn't!" And the next time he believes the lifeguard even less. But sooner or later, no matter how much struggling takes place, he gets too tired to fight any longer, and he gives up. Then he discovers to his absolute delight and amazement that the crazy stuff *will* support him. And he learns to do the dead man's float.

Now, once you have learned the dead man's float, it is easy to learn to swim. And once a man learns to die, it is easy to be born again. To give up the frantic struggle for approval, and to accept the miraculous gift of grace, opens the door for real living. But until then, life is a constant game of thrashing in the water, choking and strangling, living in a framework of basic dishonesty, surviving, if at all, by gamesmanship, politeness, and other forms of chicanery.

---

* Hezekiah 3:24. Since this is a nonexistent book in the Bible, you can quote almost anything from it.

The result of all this thrashing is that moral lines are blurred, and it no longer is possible, if it ever was, to make clear ethical distinctions. We confuse love for country with murderous warfare against innocent nations, and we break hearts and homes in the name of love. When what is called for is openness, we cry "Law and Order!" And when a good slice of discipline is needed, we slip into a well-intentioned permissiveness. The old summary of all ethical dilemmas, "Where do you draw the line?" becomes mankind's nagging and impossible puzzle. We sought to "be as God, knowing good and evil," and we have lost that knowledge altogether.

In this upside-down universe, in which no man can see clearly (because of the huge floor joist in his eye; see Matthew 7:1–5), there is no room for judgment of one's fellows. Who has the right to make it?

Instead of judgment, we must adopt a life-style built around grace. It's a so much happier and more easygoing way to live. The maxims of a judgment life-style are frantic and destructive:

What's he up to now?

Look back! Somebody may be gaining on you!

When in danger, or in doubt,
Run in circles, scream and shout! [Hezekiah 7:37]

But the maxims of grace are hopeful and full of peace:

Do not be anxious about tomorrow. [Matthew 6:34]

And the younger son said to his father, "Father, give me the share of property that falls to me." And he divided his living between them. [Luke 15:12]

In a word, when the question comes, How shall I straighten out this errant son (or husband or wife or friend or employee or parishioner), the answer is, Let him go.

For one thing, it probably isn't as big a deal as you think it is. Most of the things we worry about never materialize, and those that do are never as bad as our fantasies have painted them.

It can't do any good to worry ("Which of you, by worrying, can add one inch to his height?"), and it can do a great deal of harm. Under some circumstances it is better to relax and let the other person go on making a fool of himself, because the moment we start acting self-righteous we shut ourselves off from the only source of comfort that this world can offer: other sinful folk just like ourselves.

Of course, there will always be those who take advantage of the offer of grace. Even in St. Paul's day someone was sure to cry, "What then? Are we to sin in order that grace might abound?" It seems logical that if it is human to err and divine to forgive, then we humans must be about the business of sinning so that God can have something to do.

But that is a perversion of the doctrine. *Acceptance* is not the same as *approval*. Approval is a sort of disinterested permissiveness which whitewashes everything, or else enthusiastically supports everything, in the other fellow. But acceptance may disapprove of him entirely, while maintaining a stubborn hold on the principle of freedom: his right to go to hell if he insists on it. It is the doctrine attributed to Voltaire: "I disapprove of what you say, but I will defend to the death your right to say it."

This maxim applies not only to the freedom we permit for others, but to the respect we show for ourselves. To believe in grace means more than becoming a doormat for our wives, husbands, and children to walk upon. It means claiming for all men the respect of self, including my own self. This may result sometimes in overindulgent misuse of selfhood, but it is much more likely to succeed than a self-negation that doesn't care what happens to me or what sort of damage I do to the rest of the world.

In summary, the gospel according to Andy Capp is a gospel of accepting grace. It says to us: "You are a sinful person. Now look that fact squarely in the eye. Don't try to evade it, or you will end up with some kind of mealymouthed compromise with life. Accept yourself, with all your weaknesses and limitations, and set out to live a victorious life with that given." After all, as Andy Capp says:

Know-it-alls who have the answers for the human dilemma in easy rules are a dime a dozen. They are like the lady psychologist who claimed that anyone who followed her seven principles for child-rearing would be bound to succeed. Then she got married. Now she has seven children and no principles. There are no neat answers. Only those who have struggled in anguish through the Gethsemane of becoming persons in relationship are qualified to say. Jesus alone among men suffered the fullest agony of the gift of self, and knew what it was to be forsaken of God. But Jesus alone among men knew the meaning of joy. Likewise, only those who have known grace in the midst of sin have a right to speak on the sacred subject of marriage.*

---

* Or any other subject, for that matter.

10.

Comedy and Confession

Laughter [said the devil] does us no good and should always be discouraged. Besides, the phenomenon is of itself disgusting and a direct insult to the realism, dignity, and austerity of Hell.[1]

A funny thing happened to the human race on the way to history. The first joke had been told: light had exploded out of darkness, whales were copulating in the rolling deep, and God had painted his image on a naked, two-legged farmer named Man. And then, a funny thing happened. The Tree of Seriousness stood in the garden, and it occurred to the man (through serpent by way of wife) that if he had some of the fruit of that tree he would be able to make important decisions in ethical matters (Genesis 3:5, more or less). And he ate, and it was so. And ever since that day his problem has been that he cannot stop taking himself too seriously. What he might have done in laughter and freedom he now does by sweat and tears. Now he needs to learn to laugh again.

God will have died when laughter is extinguished.[2]

If ever the world needed a good laugh, this is the time.[3]

For God's Sake Laugh![4]

Joy is the serious business of heaven.[5]

What is humor? There are a thousand definitions, but none that explains it. It cannot be defined, any more than life can be explained. To dissect it is to kill it. So it has to be understood in terms of what it does. And one of the things it does is to bring healing through truth. Someone asked Charlie Chaplin how he was able to make people laugh, and he replied, "I tell them the plain truth of things." [6] And the truth, even though it is sometimes painful, is always friendly. It is always better to know the facts than to believe a lie. Though it hurts, the surgeon's knife exposes the infection and makes healing possible. That is why, for the Christian, confession is a healthy exercise. It isn't wallowing in sin, or feeling sorry for oneself; rather, it is looking straight at self, and accepting God's forgiveness. Confession is really the same as comedy; humility is humor. To be able to say "I'm sorry" is to be able to laugh at myself. And there healing begins.

Laughter is a weapon against all dictators, who by nature are unable to see themselves objectively. They are pompous and self-righteous, and thus they can be exorcised by laughter, as surely as vampires are destroyed by a silver bullet, or demons vanquished by the sign of the cross.

> The best way to drive out the devil, if he will not yield to texts of Scripture, is to jeer and flout him, for he cannot bear scorn. [Luther]

> The devil . . . the prowde spirite . . . cannot endure to be mocked. [Thomas More]

The stuffed shirt can't take it. Love suffers long and is kind, is not puffed up, but the person preoccupied with his own dignity is always tearing his shirt. When you can laugh at yourself, there is still hope.

Of course, there is some laughter that is merely silly, and that is not what we mean by comedy. However, even that brings us closer into the holy of holies than we might expect. Have you ever gotten so absolutely broken up that you could not stop laughing no matter how hard you tried? If so, it was probably in a place where your job depended on it, or your reputation. Radio announcers and choir singers seem to suffer from it as though it were a disease. Getting tickled in a wedding ceremony, or at high mass, is probably a reaffirmation of the seriousness of the occasion, and at the same time an underscoring of man's absurdity. It is not easy to discern the difference between nonsense and humble amusement.

But when rescued from mere frivolity, humor is a powerful force. It is, of course, the chaser that makes life's bitter drink go down easier, but beyond this it is a powerful weapon against the forces of evil themselves. It is a corrective against the pains of death and damnation, but it is also a healing force that really sets in motion their removal. It is a truism that the best comedians come out of adversity. Almost all successful comics are members of minority groups; the Jews and the blacks dominate the scene in America today. And this is not an accident. To make his life in the ghetto bearable, he learns to be amused. His laughter is born out of great misery, but he discovers that it works, and that his very simple survival technique turns out to be a weapon for doing battle with the prejudice that causes his pain in the first place.

> Aggression turned against the self seems to be an essential feature of the truly Jewish joke. It is as if the Jew tells his enemies: You do not need to attack us. We can do that ourselves . . . and even better. But we can take it, and will come out all right. We know our weakness and in a way we are proud of it.[7]

The comic who absorbs the agony of his world into his own life is a Christ-figure, one who lays down his life for his friends. Insofar as you and I are able to do this, we too survive, and when we fail to do it, something is chipped away from freedom and vitality. Jesus said, "He who seeks his life will lose it." In our context this means, "Whoever takes himself too seriously will die."

Is it not strange that in the Bible, where the word "laugh" and its synonyms and derivatives occur forty-three times, laughter is mentioned more in the Wisdom Literature* than in any other part (more than half the references)? And that the book of Job, which we associate most closely with pain and suffering, has more references to laughter than any other?

Three times laughter is on the lips of God, and in each case his attitude is one of divine amusement at the pretentions of man. Those tasks at which we set ourselves, so full of political promise or socially redeeming features, are one by one a source of amusement to the Almighty. In Psalm 2, when the nations rage and plot,

> He who sits in the heavens laughs;
> the LORD has them in derision.

In Psalm 37, when the wicked seem to be getting away with everything, growing fat and rich while the righteous suffer,

> . . . the LORD laughs at the wicked,
> for he sees that his day is coming.

In Psalm 59, the singer cries to the Lord to save him from his enemies, saying,

> But thou, O LORD, dost laugh at them;
> thou dost hold all the nations in derision.

> O my Strength, I will sing praises to thee;
> for thou, O God, art my fortress.

It is almost like the amusement of a cat playing with a mouse, as God teases the nations, which are as a "drop in the bucket" before him. He lets them have their little strut on the stage, and then whisks them off to doom (author of play chuckling in the wings).

The point is this: we ought to take God very seriously, and ourselves not at all. The schemes of men, like the best-laid plans of mice, no matter how important they may seem to us, are really

---

* The "secular literature" of the Old Testament—Job, Proverbs, Ecclesiastes, and some of the Psalms.

somewhat nonsensical when viewed from the eye of God. This is seen in reverse in the words of Paul:

> For the foolishness of God is wiser than men, and the weakness of God is stronger than men. [1 Corinthians 1:25]

The picture is like that of a swampy pool at the foot of a cypress tree. In the scum on the surface of the swamp swim all kinds of tiny life forms, each struggling to top the other and get closer to the surface. Their plans and schemes seem so important to them. But from the viewpoint of the snowy egret, sitting high in the cypress, they are all creatures of the bracken.

> What is it all but a trouble of ants,
> In the gleam of a million million suns?

Does this mean that what human beings do is not important? No, it means that what we do is not more important than it is! We have no business giving divinity to our struggles to obtain the divine. When we build towers to heaven we find ourselves scattered in all directions, speaking in confusion. Only when we wait humbly in the Upper Room does the Spirit come upon us with tongues we can understand, each in our own language. To accept this gift (which is already ours if we only look around us) is to free ourselves from pomposity and from power, and to discover the ridiculous truth that the power of God is ours as a gift. To believe that is joy and peace; to depend upon our own strength is to drive ourselves mad.

All of this is possible through the gift of one who is usually not thought of as laughing. We all know that Jesus wept, and experienced every human emotion, from tiredness, to anger, to joy. But for some reason the church has rarely depicted him as laughing. True, there have been valiant attempts to discover mirth in his teaching, such as Elton Trueblood in his book *The Humor of Christ*. He does succeed in pointing out much irony and whimsy in Jesus' dialogues with the Pharisees, his conversations with ordinary people, and his stories and epigrams. Indeed, much

of Jesus' conversation is either unbelievable or unintelligible unless
we recognize the humor in it. Trueblood cites what he calls
"Thirty Humorous Passages in the Synoptic Gospels," including
such familiar witticisms as the splinter and the log in the eye
(Matthew 7:3–4), the camel going through the needle's eye
(Matthew 19:24), and the marvelous vision of a Pharisee swal-
lowing a camel, hairy hump, hooves, and all (Matthew 23:24).[8]
But nowhere in the Bible are we told specifically about the laughter
of the Lord. By and large it has to be understood by faith, a
faith based on what we know about Jesus' celebration of life, his
affirmation of the common man, his love of nature, and his authentic humanity. If the creator of the duck-billed platypus became man, it would have to be with a sense of humor.

No doubt Jesus did laugh. Certainly he joined in the rollick-
ing songs at wedding feast and publican dinner. But we do not
remember him as a laugher, because the main business of his
life was not to laugh but to become himself an object of laughter.
He was the clown, bearing the sad visage of an Emmett Kelly,
taking on his own back the cross of human folly, so heavy a load
that we say of him, "He descended into hell." If we do not hear
him laughing it is because he allowed himself to be laughed at.
He wore the purple robe and the crown of thorns as an incon-
gruity. His whole life was a joke: a King born in a stable, a great
teacher without a schoolroom, a judge without a bench, a Messiah-
King with neither chariot nor horseman. We do not think of his
laughter because he invited us to laugh at him. He calls us to
join him in that role, to become a fool for his sake (1 Corinthians
3:18), and so to learn to laugh at ourselves.

This sounds like the craziest sort of advice. When Jesus first
gave it, men thought him mad, and crucified him as a blasphemer.
"He doesn't take God and his laws seriously enough!" they
shouted. Of course, he came to take them more seriously than
anyone ever had before (Matthew 5:17). What was really bugging
them was that he disturbed *their* dignity. God's dignity cannot be
budged! But Jesus was inviting the stuffy Pharisee, who takes his

religion so seriously, and the irresponsible pagan, who takes his sins so seriously, to laugh and weep as children again (Luke 18:17; Matthew 11:16–19). And they couldn't handle it because it meant a kind of death. For Jesus, it meant a real death, the most undignified sort, that of a common criminal, crucified on the town garbage dump. But ever since then it has been possible for another kind of death to take place—the death of pride.

> To believe in God is to be able to die and not to be embarrassed.[9]

A humorous view of self and the world is an absolutely essential corrective to the tendency to self-deification that is the ultimate downfall of man. That pride that goes before falls can only be punctured by a view of reality that will not permit us to make absolutes out of ourselves or our schemes. The voices of piosity on the one hand and paganism on the other will demand, "Get with it! Straighten up! Be serious! Wipe off that grin!" Even the theological greats stumble when they get to this point. Reinhold Niebuhr, who leads us right to the brink of celebration in his sermon on humor and faith, cannot let grace into the presence of the throne. He announces the glad release that comes to every soul who discovers laughter:

> To know oneself a sinner, to have no illusions about the self, and no inclination to appear better than we are, either in the sight of man or of God, and to know oneself forgiven and released from sin is the occasion for a new joy. This joy expresses itself in an exuberance of which laughter is not the only, but is certainly one, expression.[10]

But he cannot leave it at that. He is so conscious of the holiness of God, so sure of our human failure, so fearful of what Bonhoeffer calls "cheap grace"* that he will not let the slightest chuckle slip into heaven:

> . . . there is laughter in the vestibule of the temple, the echo of laughter in the temple itself, but only faith and prayer, and no laughter, in the holy of holies.[11]

---

* What other kind is there?

But that cannot be so! The lamb was slain from before the foundation of the world (Revelation 13:8). God is the first and the last, the beginning and the end (Revelation 21:6). Jesus Christ is the same, yesterday, today, and forever (Hebrews 13:8). He does not lose his sense of humor just because history comes to an end. He is bound to be amused for all time, at the presumption of man to come before the throne at all, and in the gladness at the prodigal's return. There is more joy in heaven, we are told, over this sort of thing than over all the pious prayers of the righteous.

And so there is Andy Capp, saint and sinner. No one can be satisfied with him as he is, but if he were anything other than what he is, he would not be human. And if he were not human, he would not be funny. And if we do not laugh, we shall not enter the kingdom of God.

> Then unexpectedly the King laughed. His body was very big and his laugh was like an earthquake in it, loud and deep and long, till in the end Ransom laughed too, though he had not seen the joke, and the Queen laughed as well. And the birds began clapping their wings and the beasts wagging their tails, and the light seemed brighter and the pulse of the whole assembly quickened, and new modes of joy that had nothing to do with mirth as we understand it passed into them all, as it were from the very air, or as if there were dancing in Deep Heaven. Some say there always is.[12]

We need laughter. Humor is honesty, and therefore a form of humility. It destroys evil, which is self-righteousness. The human race takes itself much too seriously, but God has the last laugh, and he invites us to join in.

Andy Capp is wrong. He thinks life is a cabaret. It isn't, of course. But is that any reason not to sing?

Notes

Chapter 1. UNLIKELY BEGINNINGS
  1. Quoted in *Time,* November 1, 1963, p. 71.
  2. *Ibid.*
  3. Al Capp, "The Other Capp," *Saturday Evening Post,* Mar. Apr. 1973, p. 47.
  4. *Ibid.*

Chapter 2. ANDY THE SINNER
  1. C. S. Lewis, *The Pilgrim's Regress* (Grand Rapids, Mich.: Wm. B. Eerdmans Publishing Co., 1958), p. 9.
  2. C. S. Lewis, *The Last Battle* (New York: Macmillan Co., 1956), pp. 135-140.
  3. Copyright © 1956 by Frederick Loewe and Alan Jay Lerner. Used by permission of Chappell & Co., Inc.

Chapter 3. ANDY THE SAINT
  1. C. S. Lewis, *Mere Christianity* (New York: Macmillan Co., Paperbacks Edition, 1960), p. 99.
  2. Ayn Rand, *The Fountainhead* (Indianapolis: Bobbs-Merrill Co., 1943), p. 628.

Chapter 4. THE DEATH OF JOY
  1. Ian MacLaren, *Beside the Bonnie Brier Bush* (New York: Dodd, Mead and Co., 1895), pp. 185-186.

Chapter 5. CHERCHEZ LA FEMME
  1. Herman Wouk, *The Caine Mutiny* (New York: Doubleday & Co., 1951), p. 575 .
  2. Lucretius, *De Rerum Natura,* tr. Charles E. Bennett (New York: Walter J. Black, 1946), p. 158.
  3. Wouk, *op. cit.,* pp. 272-273.

Chapter 6. HE LOVES HER, TOO
  1. Paul Scherer, *Love Is a Spendthrift* (New York: Harper & Brothers, 1961), p. 15.
  2. Thomas A. Harris, *I'm OK—You're OK* (New York: Harper & Row, 1967), p. 137.

Chapter 7. WHAT'S THE USE?
  1. Maxwell Anderson, *Lost in the Stars* (William Sloane Associates, 1950), p. 85.

Chapter 8. THEY NEED EACH OTHER!

1. Copyright © 1963 and 1964 by Bob Merrill & Jule Styne. Used by permission of Chappell & Co., Inc.

2. *The Book of Common Worship* (Philadelphia: Presbyterian Church in the U.S.A., 1946), p. 183.

Chapter 10. COMEDY AND CONFESSION

1. C. S. Lewis, *The Screwtape Letters* (New York: Macmillan Co., 1948), p. 58.

2. Martin Grotjahn, "Laughter in Psychotherapy," *Voices: The Art and Science of Psychotherapy,* Summer-Fall 1969, p. 7.

3. Jerry Lewis, "Funny Thing About Laughter. . . . ," *The Rotarian,* April 1972, p. 18.

4. The title of a book by Nelvin Vos (Richmond: John Knox Press, 1967).

5. C. S. Lewis, *Letters to Malcolm: Chiefly on Prayer* (New York: Harcourt, Brace and World, 1964), p. 93.

6. Ellis Parkinson Butler, *Our American Humorists* (Freeport, N.Y.: Books for Libraries, 1931), p. 353.

7. Martin Grotjahn, *Beyond Laughter* (New York: McGraw-Hill Book Co., 1957), p. 22.

8. Elton Trueblood, *The Humor of Christ* (New York: Harper & Row, 1964), p. 127.

9. Joseph Pintauro and Sister Corita, *To Believe in God* (New York: Harper & Row, 1968).

10. Reinhold Niebuhr, *Discerning the Signs of the Times* (New York: Charles Scribner's Sons, 1946), p. 123.

11. *Ibid.,* p. 131.

12. C. S. Lewis, *Perelandra* (New York: Macmillan Co., 1944), pp. 223-224.